OUR INLAND SEA

POEMS

OUR
INLAND
SEA

JAMES LINDSAY

A Buckrider Book

© JAMES LINDSAY, 2015

No part of this publication may be reproduced, stored in a retrieval system or transmitted, in any form or by any means, without the prior written consent of the publisher or a license from the Canadian Copyright Licensing Agency (Access Copyright). For an Access Copyright license, visit www.accesscopyright.ca or call toll free to 1-800-893-5777.

Buckrider Books is an imprint of Wolsak and Wynn Publishers.

Cover image and book design: Natalie Olsen, Kisscut Design
Author photograph: Colin Medley
Typeset in Argos by Hoftype
Printed by Coach House Printing Company Toronto, Canada

The publisher gratefully acknowledges the support of the Canada Council for the Arts, the Ontario Arts Council and the Canada Book Fund.

Buckrider Books
280 James Street North
Hamilton, Ontario
Canada L8R 2L3

Library and Archives Canada Cataloguing in Publication
Lindsay, James, 1982–, author
Our inland sea / James Lindsay.
Poems.
ISBN 978-1-928088-06-6 (paperback)
1. Title.
PS8623.I524O97 2015   C811'.6   C2015-905093-6

FOR NICOLE

CONTENTS

Our Inland Sea   11
Ghost Towns of Ontario   12
A Funnel Cloud Picks a Fight with the First Ferris Wheel   13
November Weather   14
Cinema Study   16
To Wrangle Yeti   17
What Was Left Out and What Was Seen   18
Hello, My Name is Jennifer   19
Gordon Lish   20
Zookeeper! Zookeeper!   23
Shame   24
The Common Good   25
The Golden Age of Childhood Reborn   26
A Late Moment   28
Two Photographs with Firefighters by Joel Sternfeld   29
Day Room   31
Bright Room   32
The Neighbour Hears a Music   33
"A Language is a Dialect with an Army and Navy"   34
Coney Island Aquarium   35
The Reclaimed Gold Rush Hotel   36
The Animals Here are in Uniform; Clearly, They are in Charge   37
Biologists   38
The Extinction of Flight   40

They Will Take My Island	41
Reach	42
The Interventionist	43
Photography Summer School	44
Fever Movements	45
Burn Ward	48
In Linens	50
By Definition a Collection Can Never Be Complete	51
Burglary Eulogy	52
Four Ghost Cities	54
Comedians	58
White Life	62
What Kind of Person Could Shoot a Sasquatch?	63
Past Prisoners of the Shipwreck	64
The Worms like to Be Watched	66
Perennials and Pseudocide	68
Time of the Set Table	69
Doo-Wop	70
Sound of Translation	71
Windows are the Opposite of Mirrors	72
Snowpocalypse	73
Our Inland Sea	74
Acknowledgements	77
Notes	78

LETS FIGURE OUT WHERE WE STAND
ON THE BEACH OF SOME INLAND SEA
WHICH CANNOT BE CALLED AN OCEAN.

JACK SPICER
"The Book of Gwenivere"

OUR INLAND SEA

I am told I have never truly suffered
until I father someone; have never

known a real snow because I choose to live
alongside an overlooked inland sea.

This is due to an occurrence called lake effect:
jet streams and leeward shores

beyond my control. Shelter from winter.
Yesterday's A-frame is tomorrow's yurt.

I am told Dolly Parton's arms and boobs
are covered in secret tattoos; the moon

landing was a play within a play made
to make the Russians arise and confess

to murder in front of the assembled,
and that what I believe I remember

is probably bogus, recycled stuff
told to me by old acquaintances.

Except, I can still recall the reservoir,
the urban aquarium, the public pool,

the puddle. To live by water but never
learn to swim. I am told I have never

learned to swim, so stay out of the Great
Lakes or take up the respectable practice

of getting myself noticed while drowning.

GHOST TOWNS OF ONTARIO

Deserted Gourmet Marshmallow City,
who is your master? Eighteen to thirty-five
is a long time to be a demographic, let alone a slave,
let alone a slave who spends his free time
sorting candy by colour.

Et tu, Tiny Spectre Town?
Though it's hard to get behind the line-walk you wobbled,
an officer observing the exhausted amble,
you should know no one holds that against you.
On the contrary, it's what's listed in your "What To See" section.

Ex-Radar Station Residences, why does the antique typewriter
act like a kindly mutant to toddlers? I ask because
you are the highest semi-populated point in Ontario:
500 metres above sea level, without a driver's licence
but still making the guide book every year.

At the apex the soundtrack swells into something sinister, signifying
the moment tourists discover the vacant town hall. Nothing to snicker at,
Steeltown in Decay, so do everyone a favour and think about Bartók,
one of the most important composers
of the 20th century – how Hungarian he could be,

and not be, befuddling both Americans and Nazis, who,
standing in an artificial flower shop,
deciding what to buy to lay on his grave,
choose instead to hold hands and walk the wild trillium fields
that smother what was once The Village of Childish Gall.

A FUNNEL CLOUD PICKS A FIGHT WITH THE FIRST FERRIS WHEEL

Giant feathers rocked in the air. The twenty-eight ostriches of the Midway ostrich farm bore the loss with their usual aplomb.
ERIK LARSON, *The Devil in the White City*

Czar of the midway at his war chest
sees the city sneeze as it stares
into the sun's blossom. Sol Bloom,
twenty-three and in love with the idea

of Algeria; the cutest kind of colonialism,
vaudeville's receding widow's peak
and a taste tester of Zionism. Aficionado
of indigenously nude flightless birds

combing odours from Chicago's greasy, white hair
with expensive feathers rising up against the air.
Hidden harmoniums humming from behind bushes,
blushing Tesla and, for most, the first glimpse

of electricity. Fasting artists with fans of down
performing a hoochie coochie of electricity.
Now a child sees the sea take back the castle
he had mistook for his own. The ether turning

against him like the water the lobsters were
boiled in. Winds off Lake Michigan finding a feel
for deforming metal, for peeling boas off ostriches,
for forming dark, wiggling pillars, perverts molesting

the midway, shaming I-beams to Ss. George
Washington Gale Ferris, Jr., evacuating his wheel
while the blue bullied what America made to out-
Eiffel Eiffel, baring the loss with their usual aplomb.

NOVEMBER WEATHER

Custodians tore down the tar pits
and drained the splash pads for the season.
Outside broke the lifeguards' windbreakers
who lit up the night in a shivering uprising

while armies of sweaters waited patiently
to shush their bony bodies. It was autumn.
The cold came home with a bottle of codeine.
Park swans sewed plans to become snow-

banks; trees – yawning zombies. And because
the filmmakers were kids in costumes,
they found this hilarious. Bits of Halloween
littered the streets. Shards of orange and tuffs

of faux fur were raked into mounds and set
ablaze. Still, some took in strangers for warmth.
Some mastered the art of speaking backwards.
Beaches became abandoned orphans

and everyone lined up to meet the poltergeist.
Like I said, it was autumn. It was autumn
and all bets were off. Police horses wore
blankets and developed a pesky cough.

At the fall fair we were asked to leave
for trying to teach the goats to sing.
Suddenly, it was time to vote again
and in the cynical sky zinc was seen

to surround what we came to believe
were migrations of birds forming the words
abattoir, bric-a-brac and *cul-de-sac.*
Which was strange, because we always assumed

that birds didn't understand French.

CINEMA STUDY

"When the movie starts to show you parts of itself, you know you're in trouble."
MIKE NELSON, "Laserblast," *Mystery Science Theater 3000*

A man and two robots, a gloom-gripped room,
a screen, a haze: chortle cotton in the projector's
beam boasting about it's beautiful singing voice;

drifting cherubic specs infinity left behind.
That commentary is customary is irritating,
an unnecessary audience extravagance with no

option to end. See, it's not that death doesn't
happen anymore, but unseen it seems rarer,
and around here all anyone wants to do is eat

breakfast always, lie on the fainting sofa and
make smug little statements about the seedbed.
Here, in the flickering dim they wait for annoyed

eyes, then the rest of the head to turn, a throat
clearing shushing like foam on an usher's torch.
Suppression of sound in this cold, dark room of

soft seats. So cold that petite, brief ghosts of breath
combine their whispers into a riot of shushing, rush
the projection booth and seize the projectionist,

demanding equality with oxygen. So the film flashes
back on to itself because it has nothing more to utter,
but still forty minutes to kill until the negotiator

arrives to tap the spectre's shoulder and politely
say: *Hey, those observations were tiny redeemers,
but on behalf of the rest of us, please shut the fuck up.*

TO WRANGLE YETI

Some of us had been ranting about the oysters
for months before the oysters informed us that that
was how they were suppose to taste. Finally, someone
to make the call, because who are we to think we know

anything about the telephone and its internal workings
we have never seen, but picture as perfect crystal. We sit
around all afternoon, balling up pages from each others'
chapbooks, soaking them in beer and swallowing

the pulp in lieu of food. At least someone managed
to wrangle the yeti for the expensive stunt
in the final scene. We've trained most of our lives for this,
we've lost sleep over this. See our swollen black eyes,

like we've been boxing kangaroos for food. Not that
there aren't other pressing production problems,
but the idea of missing the big kiss induces insomnia
in even the most peaceful sleepers among us. No way

of telling who's who when the next comes. One night
we will have to accept – cease struggling amongst
the sheets and accept – that it was us who let it in
by leaving the dormitory's front door open.

WHAT WAS LEFT OUT AND WHAT WAS SEEN

There was the winter the icebreakers among us
discovered that our inland sea does not fully
freeze, washing up on the shores of Wednesday
afternoon with nothing to do but sew beekeeper

suits out of seaweed, camouflage that can conceal
age, green veiled and duckbilled, growing up in dog
years, stalked by self-portraits left out online to dry.
Drying like a lakebed. An amicable divorce after a trial

separation that saw no selfish composer collapsed,
curled up on the bathroom floor with an ear pressed
to the porcelain. So cool the tile, so subtle the solo
of the faucet's constant drip, frost water skulking

through tubes, that even those who had learned
to swim when the ice gave way underneath them
had to admit that everyone seemed more bona fide
without each other's awkward boners to bother with.

HELLO, MY NAME IS JENNIFER

It's fair that that's what the yellow plastic
tag on my blue vest says, but not by choice,

it was the only one left. The other staff
blame me for forging invoices and fudging

numbers, though they are the ones hiding
under desks. I've never felt these earthquakes

that everyone's been blogging about, and not
for lack of earthquakes either, apparently.

A stuffy sightsee through the ruins proved
the inventory was off and if you don't know

how to talk to women, then you don't know
how to talk to women, no matter the language

barrier, taken tag or laws in place to regulate.
Yet the part of me that longs to condescend,

regurgitate a recently read report
to a staff I've only just met, like a mother

bird and her newly assumed nest of orphans,
is the same misogyny that will seize

an attempt at a record-setting swim
by the ankles, yank it out and declare

It's a girl! while the masked doctor, whose job
it is to slap newborns, readies himself for work.

GORDON LISH

Bag of salt. Scratched lens. Spearhead.
A cinematography magazine left out in the snow.

Haunted doghouse. Gordon Lish. Brown paper.
The neon sign blinks "psychic service" all night.

Comment section. Movie collection. Music to work to.
A new kind of plastic that feels like flesh.

Hoarders' drawers. Quick drying cement. Chipped veneer.
Paintings of lakes made to be hung in hotel rooms.

Screen cleaner. Bag of salt. Nudes.
A service that restores damaged photographs.

Feeding tubes. Commutes. Shelving.
Carrying a small mammal around in a purse.

Hippie cult. Dust mite. Diamond.
New Year's comes later and later every year.

Rock collection. Tradition. Flu season.
Tell everyone that you'll be working on your novel.

Brown paper. Swedish furniture. Brown paper.
A three-hour one-man show about Gordon Lish.

Security deposit. Smoking in bed. Synthesizer.
The last letter carrier slips on black ice.

Post-op. Post office. Caffeine.
First hundred customers get a free T-shirt.

Faux fur. Foot fetishists. Sentient machine.
Someone in a sheet with eyeholes knocks at the door.

Balsa glider. Caffeine. Caffeine.
A chance to meet others who share the same hobby.

Swamp monster. Fake Spanish. Gordon Lish.
Why some birds glide and others flap wildly.

Day job. New age. Taffeta.
Birds forgetting to migrate.

Folk art. Saxophone. Glass spheres.
A new low for plagiarism.

Reverberation. No more bananas. Modern Dance.
Never missing your favourite shows again.

Pleather. Transparent umbrella. Expensive spices.
Watching the sunrise from the new development.

Stress test. Senility. Gordon Lish.
Everyone knew that winter would never end.

Quilt. Hotline. Months that end in *r*.
Brown paper bag of salt for the walkway.

Driveway. Pageant. Blanket.
Canadian cinema of the 1980s.

Patience. Fluorescents. Carbon dioxide.
Nothing in the waiting room but piles of pillows.

Routine. Pile of ash. Greatest hits.
Poets who killed people in one of the wars.

Hula hoop. Nudes. Hair dye.
Falling asleep in the middle of the day.

Rehearsal. Synthesizer. Chrysalis.
Gordon rewriting Raymond's first book.

Music to work to. Air freshener. Wild thyme.
The alarm goes off later and later every morning.

Flu season. Deduction. Duck season.
No one has ever seen the sunrise over this city.

Too many names. Gordon Lish. Chrysalis.
Or the exit of the pillow fort in the waiting room.

Destination. Sleeping pill. Brown paper.
If they said they did, than they lied to you, Gordon.

ZOOKEEPER! ZOOKEEPER!

How long have the bars been bent?
In this light it's hard to tell what's escaped
and what's running because it's late.
A *bang* boils the ungulates. Herds
of joggers: robbers casually fleeing
the scene of the same home invasion
in different directions, at different times, and I,
wearer of the last wristwatch in the world,
do nothing to stop them. It's cowardice
that sways the superman. It's insomnia
that seduces the sleeper. My people,
white people, left the car running in the garage
and while the neighbours peeked from a cracked
curtain emergency services defused the situation.
Every night there are dining room riots
across the dinner tables of our nation,
our nation of schools and antelopes
at the watering hole agreeing out loud
I don't like to be alone
and I am alive because I am group minded.

SHAME

The exhausted mob's cries read as swarming
smarm. The snark is an extinct bird that no
preservationist laments. Taxidermists

don't call it stuffing, they call it mounting.
Who Zeus chooses to save from suffering
is as mysterious as the insignificant

insects that amass in summer's stabbings
of sunlight, awaiting the court's response
to their flea-bitten interpretation of fun.

An anxious host awaits his colleagues,
fretting over the hors d'oeuvres assembled
like riot cops kettling. The humourless

buffering wheel, the feedback loop, social
media and impending weather advance
in waves like slow sirens and Claymation,

as mysterious as the sensor readings
locked in the black box that we will need
to employ uncertain Sherpas to retrieve.

THE COMMON GOOD

I love Lovecraftian humour, father
of initial fanfiction. I love the dark

plastic domes around security
cameras. An influence so subtle

and unspoken it goes unnoticed
until American English infects

our words. The end of colour.
You may dismiss this criticism

as cynicism but remember that
it's easy to forget to laugh at the

authentic-feeling amateur frenzy.
Don't hate me for this pre-emptive

trendspotting. I love the abalone
all alone in it's mother-of-pearl

at the bottom of some channel,
waiting to be played as a conch.

Everyone has a Piggy in his or her
life, that person who makes fire

and sound. Artists experience
beat downs differently, unlike nerds

who get crushed by boulders. British
Columbia's marijuana, Puerto Rico's

chupacabra, we all do something for,
as Catholics call it, the common good.

THE GOLDEN AGE OF CHILDHOOD REBORN

reissued as docudrama,
premiered in a floating
palace where a server
politely took me aside
and whispered around
the child soldiers. I had
no opinion about the boy,
the box and the bottom
drawer full of blackout
candles, but nodded
nevertheless. On one hand,
there were the adventurous
eaters foraging from
abandoned outposts
a profusion of plants,
the kind that are allowed
to run wild in the space
between two houses.

On the other, everyone
else eating mayonnaise
sandwiches, children drafting
their own new labour laws,
passing around a queasy
privilege, everyone getting sick
at the same time, a time before
early works were honoured
on refrigerator doors. After all,
the forth and final album
will be an a cappella album,
and nobody likes that anyways
except maybe the caregiver,
who bullies the boy
with his empty box,
a bottom drawer ransacked
by tiny hands and a birthday
cake with blackout candles.

A LATE MOMENT

After the override, the order arrived, then began
the real work: offering every iris a selected testimony
but the flowers were having none of it, awkwardly
wilting their eyes away, leaving us paying in instalments,
stacking boxes in the closet. An optometrist to apologize
for the lot of them. This poem is about Afghanistan
yours is not. This childminder is Filipino
yours is not. Spotlight operators mistake squints
for sarcasm now that the truth has been proven.

Because all the choice spots in the space program
are still occupied by our beloved elders,
who get to escort the celebrities' ashes into orbit,
make money and have someone else work the Dictaphone
for once. Because we were promised degrees and drones
until retirement. We were promised patio furniture
and something like our friends' parents' future,
but for our benefit, and without the water-dwelling
deities lording over us from the bottom of the well.

TWO PHOTOGRAPHS WITH FIREFIGHTERS BY JOEL STERNFELD

Though it is their job
to spew water
on the burning house
in the background,
and I think it looks
like they are about to
(the truck is positioned
but the flames are still high),
the house will be lost,
so one breaks to browse
the pumpkin stand
in the foreground.

On the other hand,
no one ever told them
that they'd have to wet
a near-dead elephant,
exhausted by berserk,
but they do
in the background;
a sheriff's sedan
with a door ajar
on a dirt road
with psoriasis,
in the foreground.

In the photograph
with the pumpkins
it's autumn of course,
and in the one
with the elephant
it is August, I assume,
and there are actually
no firefighters in it at all,
just a man with a hose
hidden in the background,
watering the elephant
like a grey garden.

DAY ROOM

The day room is a solar cell, pure
science, light kept captive in the quietest
of solariums. A room made of windows.

A terrarium with commercial-grade carpet
and wheelchairs in rows at the start line
of the slowest race. Outside a swarm

of snowflakes are miniscule flotsam
from an exploded star raining all around.
A field of silence punctuated by coughs,

potholes roughing up the terrain. Photons
like tryptophan, filling the residents
with a great weight. The air is thick here,

makes moving thick. Nothing without effort.
Sleep creeps around the room touching
one, then another. Noon news illuminates.

A controlled burn making sure everyone's
attention is in the same direction:
toward the television and into the light.

BRIGHT ROOM

The sly light that floods my grandmother's room
is cheating: comes from a sky with no sun,
just clouds. It's grey, the light. A sharp head pain.

Her room is a hospital room, but not.
Clean and beige, buttons call a nurse if pressed,
but it's not a hospital room. Not really.

The furniture eats sound. The furniture
(bed, recliner, nightstand and the pictures,
that's it) eats sound but only from within.

Other outside sound leaks in from under
the door: a man whooping coughs, a woman
dry sobs; everyone is in their twilight.

Have I mentioned the birds? There are birds,
also grey, executing manoeuvres
outside. They make shadows flap and scatter.

A nurse asks if there is something we need.
When the door closes the window pulses.
Everything is tender: a hangover.

Then: *Is that why she didn't come Wednesday?*
When she speaks it is all soft syllables and
the sky inside smells of clean chemicals.

THE NEIGHBOUR HEARS A MUSIC

Ever since my sons moved out and foreigns moved in
I can't sleep a night to save the last of my life.

I'm not sure how many are here; always children,
and always night crying and foreign forever.

They have a music, they play it from radios
after hours, at all hours: listening slow.

They stay outside each chance they get. They hang unders!
Outdoors! They leave the baby with the old man,

as if a man our age could care for a kid. As if
men like us have extra essence. The two of them,

reliant and alone. I hear him yell in his
language for help. He's over his head I know,

I see. This is how they conduct themselves in broad
daylight, indifferent about the ones left behind.

"A LANGUAGE IS A DIALECT WITH AN ARMY AND NAVY"
After Max Weinreich

Today the last Galapagos tortoise passed away.
Tomorrow, the world's oldest throat singer.
There was a word for this, but now it's forgotten.
The old man was a dictionary, but he died in the collapse.
Linguists looked, but no one could find the door in time.
This island is sixty stories high and has many shrines.
This island of endangered nations, nations of residual lexis.
If no one understands you, you are talking to yourself.
We will think you insane to keep trying so sincerely.
We who promise to remember to remember you.
We who left you lying there unnoticed, remnants in reminisce.
Last speakers with no one to talk to and only pillows to sleep with.
Breath becomes babble, evaporates inside voices to Babel.
Only the bruised ears of shadowboxers are trained and able.
But none were found when the students came to survey.
Only ghostly mating groans in the concrete enclosure
like litter caught in the air conditioner.

CONEY ISLAND AQUARIUM

Made out of littered Zig-Zags and spit
foraged from behind the smokers' pit,

where you can find much of this sickly,
pale debris dropped by biology

students. So pale it was perfect
for forming the tank glass so kids

can watch the whale swim in his own gloom.
Somebody swapped water for Mountain Dew.

Somebody replaced the school of fish
with an AA meeting of fish.

The brochure said to expect
some listlessness, but the seals:

lying in wait for somebody
to bring them a TV so they

can get caught up on their programs.
Don't try to hide it, seals, just tell us

what you really think. With black eyes
they blink out a slow code that says

We were never mammals together.
Not us. Not you and me. No, sir.

THE RECLAIMED GOLD RUSH HOTEL

You should know that it's impossible
to remove the infected tree
without extensive damage
to the new lawn, that it's still winter
somewhere in the world,
and the production has been delayed
due to daddy issues. Which is to say
don't stay away because you feel a decision
is imminent. Sleep it off on the couch.
Time opens itself like the trench coat
of a playground pervert
if you're brave enough to wait.
A playground in the sense
that anywhere can be a playground
if you're desperate enough
to start calling every sand and gravel lot
with twisted metal and somewhere to sit
a place to play. By the way,
where is your partner
and how are the renovations
on the reclaimed gold rush coming along?
I can't wait to wake up in the camp
where a prospector breathed his last
depressed breath, danced
a final dance of mock joy,
by the muddy river that failed to reveal
precious metals, just a kind of water bug
that sparkles when it hears its own name spoken.

THE ANIMALS HERE ARE IN UNIFORM; CLEARLY, THEY ARE IN CHARGE

During dinner the house guest confessed
to feeling guilty about all the lost names
for novels never begun. He pleaded,
how can anything grow here? So near to nothing
and where the bodies are buried. I'm no shaman,
but I don't think that's how you spell *asphyxiation*.
The senator sobbed himself to sleep
in the washroom stall. The roommate, the one
who never meshed, moved out; left her chipped
dishes, melted candles and stacks of magazines.
The gun-shy stalker couldn't work up the nerve
to talk to her, and this put the audience at ease.
Young pachyderms grow their ivory privately,
hidden behind the drywall where kingdoms
are constructed out of snapped rat traps
and tough questions are asked. Oh, this?
This is a pick used in the making of masks —
the punching out of eyeholes. And that?
That is an antique woodwind from Uruguay.
Don't touch it because you don't know how to play it.
No one does. Just leave it on the cliff's edge
with the lost luggage the skycap was afraid to open
and the sea breeze will figure out its insides.

BIOLOGISTS

Listen to them squawk
in their passable pelican.
Racist, isn't it. Now know
they don't mean to mock
when their tenor's candour
slips into something more
familiar, because they blush.
Because the awkwardness.
Because the ombudsman
ought not to elect anyone
to doctor his final report
on the true expanse of all this,
whether the retriever returns
golden or not. Because erasers
irk ink, debunk debased
space expanding exponentially –
to a point. Because molecularly
speaking, we are all massive.
Huge, but mostly the hungry
space in atoms. *Mangia!*
Mangia! insists mother,
though this will make me late
for my date with the cranes.
Because without me disguised
as a swamp monster,
lurching from the brush
when they refuse to fly,
they will choose to stay
and freeze to death.

Because they have no
migratory motivation.
Because they were raised
by biologists
in white feather suits
with bird puppets on their hands.

THE EXTINCTION OF FLIGHT

All you need to do is look up and see vapour trails
to know the airplanes have returned to us.

There was a moment when we thought they had vanished
the way of the honeybee, the way of the wolves:

a rare sign of fate to see. We thought volcanic
clouds had remade flight impossible for our age,

but here they come, recurring like birthdays,
scarring the sky white, a cotton rib cage.

Our airplanes are vague villages, high places
where strangers sleep together in soft, passive rows,

touching one another by accident, rebreathing
the rumours we murmur when we are half awake.

Above bodies of water and land the atmosphere
is dense in between, holding us unseen, carrying

the unconscious across an ocean. Inside
sleepers breathe a gas of boredom, an opulence

of used oxygen remeeting lungs. All around
sounds the giant's hum deep in our chests,

deeper for us seated in coach; reminding us
that up here we are only barely aware and own nothing.

THEY WILL TAKE MY ISLAND

Weekdays since they switched the time change, so long
and beige-bright, so open
to wandering around, touching the electronics
to keep them awake.

They watch them blink on in bewilderment. Stacks
of unread books and a stove clock that strobes
the room when the curtains are closed.

And they are closed, and have been since it was
discovered that these windows work two ways.
In *and* out, like a light lock.

They get it now.

To get at it, first things first: ban all basements
and basement living, where slashes of afternoon
compete with smoke and aerosol for outside
air and inside voices. Their calls like small
animals who get in between the walls for winter.

They will take my island. They will come at it
from the rediscovered crawl spaces that
they have just started to clean.

For years they were hidden in darkness
until they cut down the trees that hid the highway
and let the commuters' constant radiance back in.

REACH

To be clear, this poem was written with the assistance
of my word processor's thesaurus and I am planning
to sue the company that made the machine that took

my fingers from me. If you can appreciate that then
I think I am ready to tell you my real name, the one
the doctor gave me in spite of my parents' objections,

the one they were ashamed of. They said it sounded too
Jewish, too much like a robot's designation. Nicknames
have never come easy to me. *Just call me Anonymous*,

I would say when asked. Which is why I was fascinated
with motors' internals, the nameless moving parts aware
of what to do without being told. To have purpose in life

like a pier reaching out to finger the horizon – but was never
intended to touch anything except water – this is how a name
can make a person's core, the part that searches for the right

words and deploys them when a panicked bystander
with a wad of paper towel rushes over and tries to stop
the bleeding, asking *why did you stick your hand in there?*

THE INTERVENTIONIST

When I still worked night shifts as an informant,
before I was pushed out by part-time photographers
and lived in the sinking house with men who owned
weapons, my family brought him to me and he began

to speak low. At first I thought he was another dumb
architect, spending waking hours staring at fact sheets
the producers compiled on us, extracted from taped
confessions. His eyes always wanting something

that didn't want to be found. Not talkative, he worked
into the afternoon. The television silenced on static
for forecasting: an angry snow, a snow on black,
a buzzing snow, snow like bees, bees bleached albino,

a hive ablaze in winter. Empty snowfields are draining,
though sometimes you see a shape surging through
the snow, a mouth releasing it's clandestine yarn,
undiscovered colours the human eye will never know,

aggressively whispering from a book he did not write,
and I learned about the sea that existed here before
I was born, history's unseen, holding out for hospice,
sculpting a script, a song structure: architecture.

PHOTOGRAPHY SUMMER SCHOOL

These camera captures were our only rain: black strips projected in reverse and dollike: costumed and posed, shimmering slick in the heat.

This was the same summer we lost control over the temperature and everyone stopped saying weather's name because we wore it like apartments.

I watched my world brown and bow, limply wilting, dehydrated by a scolding sky that had turned against us.

The fix and stop began to boil in their darkrooms, abandoned by students who refused to enter the chemical ovens, fuming with tools.

We walled up the dead darkrooms, infected sinuses in the house's head, and we walled up ourselves from the heat in front of fans' oscillations.

Our speech pulsed through the murmuring blades, mechanizing our words until we were a room of robot voices discussing escape plans.

We hung the brittle negatives, decaying husks, hung them like we used to hang snakeskins from the ceiling beams for luck.

FEVER MOVEMENTS

All I have is the will to remember. Time revoked/fever dreams — I wake up reaching, afraid I'll forget...

....

Fever — that time burning. I want to go with the music — spin, fall with it.
JAMES ELLROY, *White Jazz*

You came with hot chills
and cold sweats. Neither here
nor there,
like smoke's shadow
you moved across my body in influence
and out my pores and down my neck,
sticking to the sheets, killing
my sleep, but not the movements that
sound more like music than
music has ever sounded.

*

Acetaminophen eases
the aching waiting
on a promised solstice.

Until then: a novel
with no chapters
and an article

about debt that
your aunt emailed
you before this started.

*

There's a drop of red on your sleeve
from that time you faked your own death,
but that's not important.

*

The discovery that we could make flame
was also the discovery that skin
will blister when connected with flame.

And we learned to long for prepackaged ice,
to push ourselves to stand up. Just because
you can't move, doesn't mean you don't have to.

*

The people across from you are playing that game
where one person closes their eyes
and describes something (usually
it's an object, but now it's sounding
like she's talking about an emotion
or feeling or something) while the other
person tries to draw it,
asking simple questions:
Where does the right side start to curve?
How long are the waves again?
What kind room would it live in?
Etc.?

*

Lying on the makeshift bed
I pretend to die for the medical students
who look at me with eyes of forged concern
and ask before touching.

*

Caressed by rhythm
that keeps time by the beat of
erratic hands tapping
out a faint white jazz
that presses the skin as if it were
red silk scarves held by dancers
in some recital performed
in a sweat lodge that doubles
as a waiting room.

*

Part of the problem is that I keep confusing
you with me and me with we. It took years
to get here and I can't imagine doing it again.
I'm an idiot, ignorant of the true patients.
It's my privilege: my mumblecore-mancold
that excuses stealing from better writers.

*

Don't let it get out of hand next time
see the signs
take a pill. This time
it came on like carbon monoxide,
though next time

BURN WARD

Behind safety glass, children afraid of fire
do an imaginary dance up and down
the walls of their suburban basements.
They lick everything out of reach. Seared
hands move like charmed snakes. The smoke
agitates the air until it turns against them.
Smell carbon, burning: a stroke or a seizure,
something unseen and internal. They have
a real feel for flames as some empathize
with animals. They live on the building's
cliff face. Some nights the birds go
kamikaze at it's high, invisible windows.

Glass is not a liquid, maybe never was.
Their bodies become broken embers
discovering free fall as flying. Redbird matches
are the best, burn like long, slow wicks.
Those Christmas lights will never come down.
Staying up all year blinking, blinking. When
I think of them now I think of sparks sparking,
think of them flicking the flint of the lighter,
pressing it to the flowering yellow wallpaper.
It was then they finally grasped life. Consuming
carnivorously, breeding between the walls
and floors, spreading like secrets spoken

in silent hospitals where I have spent seasons
visiting wild mutes who do not believe
that they can't speak. Instead they slither
and hiss and the hiss melts things not made
of metal. You must bleed your radiators
at least once a year or they won't ever
get warm. So hot it felt cold. By then it
was already burnt. And the burn-ward's
children still dancing, wringing their hands
to fling the feeling out, birds learning to flap
their wings, not because they desire to fly,
but because they've been pushed from behind.

IN LINENS

There are people who are paid well to keep an ear out for virus noise: the dripping faucet of the interspecies jump; the animals in the walls of sick people on airplanes; and in a different sense, the linen-white noise of the oscillating fan that we can't sleep without. Listen,

these people, these people are not like you and me. These are the people at parties, who take your hand, lead you to the laundry room, lock the latch and proceed to put you to sleep with stories of all the answering machines they found in the second-hand stores. "No one thinks to erase the tapes.

No one thinks someone will be there to listen. No one." And acetate, anti-Semitic as it is: "the only true sound storage," and Edison cylinders, and "chalk's rise was due to its lack of permanence." It's all you can do to slouch there, compulsively swallowing to stay awake. It's at times

like these that you become acutely aware that your Adam's apple is actually the last Prussian in disguise, that this is a system of counting based on the number three, so don't discount the bacteria that lines our insides in linens, they're not so hot on being here either.

BY DEFINITION A COLLECTION CAN NEVER BE COMPLETE
After . . . *I Listen to the Wind that Obliterates My Traces* by Steve Roden

Any good collector must be willing to change,
adapt and eventually purge their old tones
as the rage changes, as the collector changes,
shedding commemorative platelets into plastic

sleeves, stacked in storage units, to be sold
on eBay. If seen correctly the collector appears
in mosaic when viewing the collection
from the catwalk or observation deck.

The collection regards a room like a ghost
regards a room. There's little difference
between yawning and singing other than intent.
The collection regards the collector like cave paintings

regard rock. It's not that there are more colours now
than eighty years ago, we just have better, newer names
today. It took decades to comprehend the comma,
let alone the semicolon. But that's what they want—

all the headstrong young collectors, drunkenly mapping
new neighbourhoods by night on bikes without lights: to be
the ones that get to name the new colours. *Athletes*
in the loose sense, *compulsive* in the strict, gathering

what they thought were shotgun shells, but in reality
were empty prescription bottles that held sea sounds.
The collection should reflect all separations,
massaging directions stressed by the winds

that obliterate the collector's traces.
These winds will thin the collector's nature,
like another wind would whisper to a runner's
lungs, coaching: *In, out; less, more.*

BURGLARY EULOGY

Everyone remembers the local prowler
who used our own ladders against us, ladders
left leaning like offerings in alleys. Who could
forget how he sauntered himself up the rungs,
seeping through trustfully cracked windows.

Surely no one cannot picture him cross-legged
on our kitchen floors, going through our junk drawers.
We'd find miniature manifestos weeks later
tucked between cutlery, written in pig Latin.
But what was it that the police profiles missed?

When did we discover ourselves finding these
intrusions endearing? Remember his strange
middle name better suited for a horse? The only
inconvenience was not knowing what was stolen,
though we all felt it. "Felt it" as in phantom limb.

When filling out reports we tended to leave
that part blank. I myself used to steal single
pages from library books just to get at their
word grit, deeply creased in the narrow folds.
If the City can forgive me for that then. . .

Or the lost languages he was trying to save,
how he'd ask the accented for written scraps
of their disintegrating tongues and slip them,
word grit and all, into that classic smock pocket
he was so known for. "We lose a language

every fortnight," he was fond of saying. "One day
AM radio disappears, the next, bees forget
what their dances mean." And who can forget
those always welcome hand drawn bills he posted,
advising new neighbours to walk "Egyptian-Style"

and against the traffic when walking at night.
I want be the one to say *godsend* or *concierge*,
but I'll leave that to the press. For the moment let's
remember him in patchwork on the park's public
bulletin board, in those newspaper tearings

we've all culled over the years and stored in files
initially intended as evidence, but quickly
those boxes became hope chests and began to fill
our apartments room by room, as if tourists
learning what we do where we live – casing us.

FOUR GHOST CITIES

1.

Reverse ruins waiting for urban puberty
the green bud of middle class to swell in them.

The homes of the future have been born fully grown
gangs of unfilled cement and glass oafs, standing
by their lonesome for years, awkwardly
waiting to be named, regarding
their bloodless muscles with wonder, like an infant
with their genitals, who sees potential
but remains powerless for the next ten years.

2.

Patience is an empty parking lot, a cello solo
to a hollow, an implied people as yet unmet.

The young cities stand self-conscious.
Embarrassed, they keep as quiet as new concrete
hoping the world won't notice their hanging
heads, filled with a populace of wandering realtors
and wind, blushing when the West sneers in fear
of the images the satellites send back:
your braces and your bad skin; your father
posing in his walk-in gun closet,
arms crossed and chin up, letting a smile slip.

3.

*Rhetorical apartment blocks talking to themselves
instead of singing for their inconceivable citizens.*

Perfect servants, but before that, drunken uncles
slumped in the open doorway, letting the cold air in,
pretending not to notice their worker-maker relations
pulling on their pant legs and hiding under their robes
like the emaciated children of Scrooge's second spirit,
we will never hear from them again, their hem
is two rooms, eight others and sharing a bed with a stranger.

4.

Who will be the first to inhabit an unused empire
and how will the last human alive ever be sure?

A vacant Rome erected every two months
to forbearance and for employed pioneers
who are willed to people the gods' gambles
but not before anyone else and not
if they can't be convinced that the almost total silence
that dampens their thoughts will not obscure them
completely, leaving an accountant alone and mayorless
to roam around the promise, waiting on the rest to arrive.

COMEDIANS

Comedians as people who still collect stamps.
Comedians as Saskatchewan.
Comedians as the summer you discover yourself.
Comedians as improvisational skills.
Comedians as the actor who plays two roles.
Comedians as the hesitant doctor and the troubled daughter.
Comedians as an Academy Award-winning film on liquor.
Comedians as screaming at a child out of anger.
Comedians as public school teacher purgatory.
Comedians as magazines in a waiting room,
    and the furniture in the waiting room as well.
Comedians as a ticket for loitering.
Comedians as a suicide note.
Comedians as hostage negotiators.
Comedians as anxious historians.
Comedians as caregivers in a hospice hospital.
Comedians as the unsung heroines of British literature.
Comedians as volumes two and five,
    but not one, three or four.
Comedians as last speakers, and later, as lost languages.
Comedians as the world's five smallest nations.
Comedians as, in no particular order, the Vatican,
    Nauru, Tuvalu, San Marino and Monaco.

Comedians as Princess Grace at her coronation.

Comedians as Tropical Storm Jean.

Comedians as strangers who yell insults at you from passing cars.

Comedians as both *F* words and the *N* word as well.

Comedians as damning evidence.

Comedians as diplomatic immunity.

Comedians as the insanity defense.

Comedians as the cure for cancer,

> but only brain cancer.

Comedians as the cause of autism.

Comedians as amnesiacs.

Comedians as asthmatics.

Comedians as the perfect alcoholics.

Comedians as an aspic salad.

Comedians as the death of irony,

> or at least what gives irony cancer.

Comedians as the last smoking section in this city.

Comedians as the fake fire escape that will be the death of us all.

Comedians as serrated blades.

Comedians as stainless steel that has been stained.

Comedians as Jazz Nazis judging your taste.

Comedians as the noble tradition of male sopranos.

Comedians as the best airplane food you ever had.

Comedians as twin-engine Cessnas.

Comedians as "Unidentified aircraft, identify yourself."

Comedians as what the people of Saskatchewan thought they saw in
    the sky.

Comedians as urban legends proved true.

Comedians as the Albino Alligators' Rights Movement.

Comedians as three-legged dogs just glad to be hobbling at all.

Comedians as a play about animals and as the animals as well.

Comedians as pets you've come home to.

Comedians as amateur ornithologists sneaking into the aviary after hours.

Comedians as a stuffed shark hung above the dinning-room table,
    where an eccentric billionaire has assembled a group of strangers
    who have something in common.

Comedians as what's on the fourth floor,
    where the guests have been forbidden to go.

Comedians as all the characters from Kafka's *The Trial*, except for K.

Comedians as true crime stories.

Comedians as the soundtrack for a video of machines grinding things,
    sparks.

Comedians as a watercolour of a Saskatchewan sunset,
    hung on a hotel room wall.

Comedians as conceptual curators of the controversial installation
    Five Different Kinds of Sand on the Floor.

Comedians as "Please don't disturb the sand. Thank you."

Comedians as Andy Warhol's *Red Car Crash*, from the Death and Disaster Series.

Comedians as carsick highway patrol officers.

Comedians as the only drunk driver you feel comfortable being driven by.

Comedians as either take the ride or walk home in the dark.

Comedians as opening the front door and not recognizing where you are.

Comedians as the nagging feeling that you should find this familiar, but you don't.

Comedians as knowing that something old is hidden under the floorboards.

Comedians as not knowing how you know that something old is hidden under the floorboards.

Comedians as all the ball bearings rolling to the sinking side of the house and finding the hole missed by the naked eye.

WHITE LIFE

When I yell, know it's not you who
I want to hear me. Vodka, Kahlúa
and milk are occasionally called a
Caucasian! Is there anything more
Canadian than not acknowledging
an amputation? I have friends
who would disagree, clueless to
the vagueness of daylight and
working drunk. I'm sorry, Céline Dion,
but that's not how you're supposed to
vocalize. Just sit there while I
summarize last week's episode to
you. She's twitchy and likely to
nap when it's not about us. I'm sorry
that nothing notable happened today.
Maybe tomorrow, after my flaming
leap through the sugar glass and the
stunt coordinators suffocate the fire
that I like to think I'll light myself.

WHAT KIND OF PERSON COULD SHOOT A SASQUATCH?

A social class that spends days perusing
hardcover catalogues, while the civil war,
well into its second year, rages on
underwater, where cannons are arrogant
whales and soldiers send home photographs
of others who resemble them enough to let
their loved ones imagine that the images
they kiss are alive, but being underwater,
are ignored by air and filled with fear
of the day when the crew from the show
about people like them will arrive and politely
ask to touch the part of the brain that senses
burning. Offering nothing when asked,
what kind of person could shoot a sasquatch?

PAST PRISONERS OF THE SHIPWRECK

Every time there's a piano around some excited
Luddite must prove that it can still be played,
and every time there's intent, talk breaks it by blabbing
over the quiet crowd and old-timey music. So concludes
the selected lectures on the difference between lecterns,

podiums and other things hands rest on
to keep from fidgeting. Feel free to now throw
open the curtains and discard the unused
drafting table. It underwhelms since this CD
of whales singing arrived. Books loaned out for years

are also making a comeback, though the shelves
are now occupied with what was found on the return
trip from the dump, which is mostly other books
and bits of beach glass, patiently soothed by the sand
that is in love with the great lake,

that is in love with the shipwreck,
that is the seed in the deep song sung,
chanted really, by public drunks to keep from
crying the whole way home on the night bus.
Why do they stop singing when professional

entertainers board? That's rhetorical,
of course, but if there's something here to be learned,
it's the polished metal in the shipwreck that glimmered.
Past prisoners used it as a makeup mirror
and to snort sand off of, not, as one would think,

for spying around corners on the young guards,
still fresh from the showers, both sexes glistening,
so obviously wet, shaking up all kinds of disgust
and arousal in an aerosol sprayed directly to the face.
Good then that the available ventilators were made of

pages from magazines hidden under the bed,
and whatever lumber the great lake would let them take.
This way their gaze went uninterrupted by chemicals
and the intercourse they were expected to take part in,
making their sentence somewhat easier to sit out.

THE WORMS LIKE TO BE WATCHED

I've read your blog and call bullshit
on it. Who are you to choose moods
for my hot bod. If I exude gluten
through my tear ducts and you
can't stand my yeasty weeping,
close your eyes and imagine you're
in bed. How dare you spit on the rest
of the nest just because you flew first.
Look around, do you see anyone else
holding hands here? How can it
be debatable that we've all turned?
What's the word for when you want
to show off some skin, but are afraid
of being burnt by an angry
sun god? Ask modern archery
about her doohickeys, compound
bows, how they forced us to forget
our lethal instincts. She'll explain
that questions are like pagan rites:
satellite worship for Cro-Mags,
primates winking at orbitals,
the moon, craft above our planet
made of earth. And all the while,
underneath the soil somewhere,
worms have sex indiscriminately,
unconcerned about opinions
or who would want to observe
their most primordial romance.

As a matter of fact we enjoy
being watched, the worms inform
the obstetricians, peaking out
from behind a curtain. Knowing
this, bravado joins the voyeurs
tête-à-tête, asking for a more
compelling post-coital cry from
the newly coupled life partners,
squirming around passionately
on a ball of mud spinning in space.

PERENNIALS AND PSEUDOCIDE

Humbled graduates huddle
in an igloo atop a mountain
made of empty oxygen tanks
and climbers' corpses, contemplating
the calculus of their defunct
compasses, the blind math made
wild by magnets with wings,
the brilliant few who saw through
the fluke: kids and their flare gun
fights, bears who have been taught
to operate cameras, sleeping dogs
who hunt in dreams, their twitching
limbs unemployed with the best possible
pessimism, the worrying affect
of afternoon alcohol preserved in pantries
of the reptilian brain, where a restaurant
serves an animal rarely eaten,
typically found on the side of the road,
without migration there'll be more of these
frozen orphans and other ever-present
phenomena found in minor groups,
be it connoisseur or school shooter –
it's impulse the young puppeteers
shy away from, envying those who have
what it takes to fake their own deaths
and start again in a new neighbourhood
with a fresh face and clever pseudonym.

TIME OF THE SET TABLE

Take a knee for a moment and consider cancer
as social contract instead of conspiracy theory
to explain the innate hatred of one's own voice,

as heard by microphones concealed in the chandelier,
after the ceremony but before the deceased
caretaker moped around the haunted ballroom.

This is the time of the set table:
the reconsideration of the salad fork
as a social class of eating disorders;

the cutlery predicted in science fiction
we collect to fuck ourselves with, a nick
in the skin that will never stop bleeding,

a pint taken in pinpricks in consideration
of sugar and standing up too fast, atrophied,
bedsores, backbreaking bedroom boredom.

Key here is understanding agoraphobes
measuring coastlines by an afternoon's algorithm,
the over-educated sequestered in duvet caves

mined by illiterate librarians
who introduce themselves as friends
when met in the dark, down tunnels of the comforter.

No ordinary acrobats ignoring
a scented candle setting off the smoke detector,
no run-of-the-mill fire drill at the ape sanctuary,

therefore, another dishwater decade
of "stop, drop and roll" and crawling on all fours
toward the light, where the exit is ajar,

and there is air to be had by all, hands to hold
and someone smarter who knows how to work
the computer that controls the time of day.

DOO-WOP

Capital is eternal, the Internet is forever, and corporations can last a very long time.
ALEX GOOD, "Shackled to a Corpse."

My problem with most New Age Christian mystic
cults is that there's not enough ululating. Now,

deep in the underbelly of the Internet, YouTube,
I find one with an impressive amount of ululating,

and it's almost too much. Yodeling like an auctioneer-
speaking-in-tongues-sound-tapestry of blackened onions.

Lobsters have no known lifespan and some types
of octopuses "decorate" their dens. I don't know

how I know this but I've known it forever. Some
"people" are too big to fail, so for the sake of the state

that governs its arts under the tyranny of Margarets,
they must be coddled. The orator Elizabeth Clare Prophet

hated rock music and unsuccessfully predicted doomsday,
but was loved by a family that, she claimed, at their peak,

was a hundred thousand strong. An eternal capital
too big to fail until the spiritualist's body does not ascend:

Sir Arthur Conan Doyle's collection of ghost and fairy
photographs; the rise and fall of parapsychology;

a website devoted to the cataloguing of abandoned house
interiors; a pamphlet I found on a bus seat about

red herrings that surround us, touching on every area
of our daily lives, subtly harmonizing in perfect polyphony

an indistinguishable frequency. Not that this noise is secret;
things so enormous don't have to be to go overlooked.

SOUND OF TRANSLATION

Before this peasant food, recognize the knack
brought back from sound and assumption,
post-punk parasite. Once more, and this time
with feeling. Your nostalgia's reminiscent

of Plexiglas flexi discs, sound of scratch,
sound of scuff, sound of impossible
repetition, reptilian trueness,
two complete cycles mistaken as twins.

Inconsiderate twins: from this to that,
then never again. Pop, hiss, then silence.
Empty uhs and ums. Placeholder's facial
blindness. Yesteryear, we can hear you,

but barely. Can you clear your throat?
The hour's second's mucus. The sound
of chlorophyll slinking out of cell walls.
The assumption that autumn is final.

Forgetful defibrillator, cylinder transcriber,
cassette components collapsed across
the back of a sick stead at the gates
of the tape head. From this to that,

then never again. Let the tourists name
the streets, landmarks, calls of the local
wildlife locals no longer notice.
The sound of translation broken by time,

balanced by the decaying light of bulbs,
burnt out over a thousand years ago.
The sound of the salvage machine reaching.
The assumption of exits and endings.

WINDOWS ARE THE OPPOSITE OF MIRRORS

I'm organizing a field trip to The Museum
of Windows of the World. I hear that if you look
through them you will see what they saw
when they were part of a wall, the shimmering
lens skin that records a building's vista, every
bright sky and bird strike they looked out on.
In addition, the optical wing features famous
frames presented as if in their natural settings,
when they were part of a face – mounted on wax
heads made from the death masks of miniature
dead moons. There is a witness encased in the silica.
Scientists, extracting the translucent cinema
caught in the invisible, all that they learned
is that this process can not be reproduced
in mirrors. Mirrors hold our facial refuse tight,
unwilling to let go. Like metal in the microwave,
their elements are resistant to our impatience.

SNOWPOCALYPSE

The pernicious rise of poptimism
irritating radio-rhizome's roots,

shape-shifters on another smoke break,
the anti-vaxxers all revved up over

cola control, but haven't "we" fucked
up this district enough? Field recording,

found footage, POV – O SeaWorld, my
SeaWorld, in Ontario we call you

Marineland and the grape growers feed
the orcas icewine. Cold snap, look inside

my synthesizer and see electricity
lying about flying a creaking vessel

that does not want to dock. Mournful
moan of an incomplete combination.

Bassoon, bass oboe, in Boston they are
digging out. Lawyer up. Meet the hundred

people hoping to live and die on Mars.
An empire built on sugar, slave money

circulating still to this day. Moustache
wax in the vox. The tacky colours came back

because they couldn't live without us in heck
body shaming the snowman as he melts,

who's death we are still obliged to avenge
even if it means taking an unpaid position.

OUR INLAND SEA

You know I can't play your keyboard (though
I've been told I have the mean, twiggy fingers

of a pianist) any more than I can breaststroke
the great lake (though I've been told I have a

swimmer's body: emaciated, but ropy
with elastic muscle and buoyant sinew), still

you ask me to cash in this hand-carved currency
at some lemonade stand or another. The boy's

baffled face, reflected in a pitcher of sweet lemon
water and ice – if only you could have seen this

then maybe you would stop picking at my
penmanship and for once say something nice

about my skin – which, to be fair, feels like it has
been dried and stretched into one of those horrible

lampshades that are so in with eccentric collectors
and British royalty. I'll be the first to admit I have

no idea how to talk to the children of today. By ten
they have already been forced to raise, then flush

entire families of goldfish. You can see this
in their war-torn little eyes. You can see this

in our inland sea, full of koi, grown flushed guppies,
so numerous that astronauts know them and the zebra

mussels that razor-wire our shore, biting like spiteful
pets as we wade out of the forgivable years society

seems not to notice. Not because it isn't affordable –
it isn't fashionable to be seen with hands so capable

at cracking open tiny striped shells of an invasive
species from southern Russia – where I hear pornography

originates, the birthplace of rivers. And, as we know,
rivers are rapists, like bees with flowers. So then islands

hate rivers more than we hate those who haven't read
the collected works of our inland sea. Which are back

in print and are okay. Okay in the way things are
comme ci, comme ça now that we're all allergic

to most food. Like an airplane from the island airport
with a blown hatch, its people sucked out and snowing

over the winter water: empty but airborne
and full of electronics that work perfectly.

ACKNOWLEDGEMENTS

"Day Room" and "The Neighbour Hears a Music" were originally published in *Taddle Creek*; "Fever Movements" in *Prairie Fire*; "Biologists" and "The Reclaimed Gold Rush Hotel" in *The Humber Literary Review*. Thank you to the editors.

This book is dedicated to Nicole Dawkins, who believes in me more than I ever knew was possible.

Many thanks to: Ann Lindsay and Willy J; Steve and Maria Dawkins; Beth Webster.

Thanks to everyone involved with Pleasence for your friendship and support.

Thanks to Jeff Latosik, Derek McCormack and Miranda Pearson for their consideration and comments on some of these poems in their infancy.

Special thanks to Paul Vermeersch for his mentorship and long, long-standing support.

Finally I would like to thank the Ontario Arts Council and Toronto Arts Council for their financial support.

NOTES

"A Funnel Cloud Picks a Fight with the First Ferris Wheel" The epigraph describes an incident that took place on July 9, 1893, when a windstorm struck the World Fair in Chicago, stranding passengers on the first Ferris wheel. Designed by George Washington Gale Ferris, Jr., it was made to "out-Eiffel Eiffel," and was essentially a retort to Paris' Exposition Universelle of 1889. A twenty-three-year-old former vaudevillian named Sol Bloom, "czar of the midway," curated the fair with exotic pavilions that featured Algerians, belly dancers, Tesla's demonstrations of electricity and ostriches among many other things.

The "Two Photographs with Firefighters by Joel Sternfeld" are: "McLean, Virginia, December 1978" and "Exhausted Renegade Elephant."

"A Language is a Dialect with an Army and Navy" is a quip coined by the sociolinguist and Yiddish scholar Max Weinreich.

"They Will Take My Island" was written for Paul Vermeersch's blog that features various poets' interpretations of the Arshile Gorky painting of the same name.

"By Definition a Collection Can Never Be Complete"... *I Listen to the Wind that Obliterates My Traces* is a book by the artist Steve Roden that displays part of his collection of early photographs related to music (anonymous African-American guitar players, one-man bands, crafters of homemade instruments displaying their inventions) and rare 78 rpm recordings compiled on two CDs. The photographs are paired with his own meditations on collecting and quotes from Hamsun, Wordsworth and Nabokov. "I Listen to the Wind that Obliterates My Traces" is also a line from the Pär Lagerkvist poem "Aftonland."

"Four Ghost Cities" Western media has reported that the developers in China are building entire cities faster than they can be populated in order to keep up a high GDP rate. In addition, many of the residential areas in these "ghost cities" are unaffordable to all but the most affluent, meaning that the workers who build and maintain the cities cannot afford to live there. They instead commute from surrounding areas, many of which suffer from overcrowding and outdated infrastructure.

"Doo-Wop" The epigraph is taken from an essay by Alex Good, titled "Shackled to a Corpse: The Long, Long Shadow of CanLit," which appeared in *Canadian Notes & Queries* (issue 92, Spring 2015). Good argues that Canadian literature resists moving beyond it's cultural boom of the 1960s, creating an establishment, as referred to by Richard Rosenbaum, whom he quotes, as the "Tyranny of the Margarets" in the introduction to *Can'tLit: Fearless fiction from* Broken Pencil *magazine*.

Elizabeth Clare Prophet was the founder of the Church Universal and Triumphant, whose sermon "Invocation for Judgement Against and Destruction of Rock Music" was popularized on the album *Sounds of American Doomsday Cults*, volume 14, and has been sampled by several musicians. An example of the CUT's "ululating" can be found at www.youtube.com/watch?v=Y6LqZOfnngg ("Church Universal And Triumphant, Inc. Featuring Elizabeth Clare Prophet - Decree 10.05").

"Snowpocalypse" "The pernicious rise of poptimism" is taken from the title of a *New York Times* article by Saul Austerlitz, published on April 4, 2014.

The line "a creaking vessel that does not want to dock" is from Beniffer Editions' description of *Aulos' Second Reed* by Part Wild Horses Mane on the Tomentosa website.

JAMES LINDSAY has been a bookseller for more than a decade. He is also co-owner of Pleasence Records in Toronto, a record label specializing in post-punk, odd-pop and avant-garde sound pieces.